Impacting Your World One Earthling at a Time

ALIEN INVASION

Impacting Your World One Earthling at a Time

A creative study of the book of Ephesians

by Michael Warden

Illustrated by Scott Angle

Standard Publishing
Cincinnati, Ohio

TABLE OF CONTENTS

Cover Illustration by Scott Angle
Inside design by Dina Sorn
Edited by Dale Reeves

© 1998 by Standard Publishing
All rights reserved
Printed in the United States of America

The Standard Publishing Company, Cincinnati, Ohio.
A Division of Standex International Corporation.

| 05 | 04 | 03 | 02 | 01 | 00 | 99 | 98 |
| 5 | 4 | 3 | 2 | 1 |

HOW TO USE THIS BOOK

A scientist named J. Robert Oppenheimer once said, "The best way to send an idea is to wrap it up in a person." The Christian term for that is *incarnation*. It means "in the flesh," and it describes an "alien" invasion that happened over 2,000 years ago—when God invaded history by sending his Son, Jesus.

The apostle John described the invasion this way: "The Word became flesh and made his dwelling among us . . ." (John 1:14). That invasion not only changed the course of history, it also accomplished something stunning and unexpected. When Jesus entered the human world, he established a whole new race of people—a new breed of aliens forged out of the human population. As this breed is transformed by the power of God into a totally new creation, John says they become children of God: "children born not of natural descent, nor of human decision or a husband's will, but born of God" (John 1:13).

All of us were born human, with human traits and worldly desires. For most of us, it wasn't until a little later in life that we placed our faith in Jesus, and were thereby transformed into a new kind of being. Now we are no longer just humans, even though we still wear a human skin. In the truest sense, we have become aliens in the world. Because of Christ's invasion into our lives, this world is no longer our home. We are still in it, but we are not "of" it. Instead, we are now "of" Christ. We are members of his body and citizens of his kingdom.

Still, it's hard to forget our old "human" ways. After all, we still look human (most days, anyway). And our old human traits and passions have been ingrained in us since childhood, making them easy to fall back into.

That's why the apostle Paul wrote the book of Ephesians. The Ephesians were young "aliens" who were indescribably rich in Christ, but they were living as spiritual beggars because they were ignorant of their new identity. In the first three chapters of Ephesians, Paul describes how Christ's "invasion" into the world brought unparalleled spiritual wealth and treasure to those who believe in him. Paul reminds the Ephesians not only of who they were before Christ came, but also of who they are now because of Jesus' impact in their lives.

In chapters four through six, Paul turns the invasion outward, explaining how his readers can live effectively as "aliens" in the world, teaching them ways in which they can impact humanity for Christ.

This book is designed to help you challenge your teenagers with the truths contained in Paul's letter to the Ephesians—and discover how to start an "alien invasion" in their own lives and world.

Each session in this book is divided into three sections: **Sightings, Close Encounters** and **Life Invasion.** Each of these sections contains more than one option or activity for you to use, depending on your needs and the needs of your students.

In the **Sightings** section, two creative ideas are provided to help you introduce the topic to your group. Typically, one idea is more active than the other. Choose whichever option you think would work best with your kids.

In the **Close Encounters** section, you'll find three Bible activities that will help your kids creatively explore specific sections of the book of Ephesians. The first two activities in this section are designed to work together as an experiential study of the Scripture, combined with interactive small-group debriefing and application. The third activity is typically less active and uses real-life quotes or stories to encourage discussion about the Scripture and its application to daily life. You may choose to do only the first two activities, just the third or all three—depending on your time limitations and the needs of your group. Remember, "the lesson was made for man, not man for the lesson."

In the **Life Invasion** section, two closing options are provided to help your students take what they've learned and immediately apply it to their lives. The first option uses a variety of approaches to help solidify the learning. The second option offers students a more specific challenge each week for applying what they've learned to their lives in a practical way. Feel free to select the closing that's most appropriate for your group.

Bruce Cockburn once wrote, "We are lovers in a dangerous time. Nothing worth having comes without some kind of fight. We have to kick at the darkness until it bleeds daylight." In the book of Ephesians, Paul explains how God has made us supernatural "lovers" in Christ, and he describes the joys and dangers of reaching out with that love to a human world. You can use this course to teach your students about that love—a love that has transformed them into new creations, and a love that can inspire them to launch a fresh invasion for Christ into their world.

AWESOME ABDUCTIONS

In this session, your students will transform each other into "aliens" to discover how it feels to be different from everyone else in a crowd. Then they will redo their transformations based on the description of our transformation in Christ found in Ephesians 1. Through this experience, they can discover how God has transformed them from "ordinary humans" into totally new creations in Christ.

Sightings

ALIEN TRANSFORMATIONS

Once everyone arrives, form groups of five or fewer. Set out the supplies and say, **"I believe that aliens are living among us on earth. In fact, I think there are several aliens in this room right now. And I can prove it!"** Have each group choose a team captain, then say, **"Aha! Now we know who some of the aliens are! That's because aliens can't resist the opportunity to be team captains! (I know this because I read it in *The Star* just last week.) Now we can expose you aliens for all to see."**

Instruct the team members to use the supplies you've provided to transform their team captains into aliens. Tell them to make the transformations as wild as possible, so everyone can see their true "alien" identity clearly. Encourage teams to assign specific attributes to their alien, such as "he has the ability to fly," or "she normally lives underwater," and encourage them to decorate their "alien" accordingly.

When teams are finished, let each team present their alien and explain his or her attributes to the rest of the group. Then have them discuss these questions in their teams:

• **How does it feel to be an alien among humans?**
• **Why do aliens always try to hide their true identities?**

Congratulate the teams on their creative work, then have the "aliens" remove their costumes. Conclude by saying, **"Although we're poking fun at the idea of 'aliens living among humans' in this activity, there is a different sort of 'alien' that the Bible talks about. This race is called Christian, and if you've trusted Jesus to**

LESSON TEXT
Ephesians 1:1-23

LESSON FOCUS
Jesus wants to radically transform our lives.

LESSON GOALS
As a result of participating in this lesson, students will:
• Experience what it feels like to be an alien.
• Discover why Jesus wants to transform humans into aliens.
• Discuss how Jesus' transforming power might impact their lives.

Materials needed:
Newsprint; foil; tape; markers; makeup; other miscellaneous costume items

Check This . . .
When teams present their "aliens" to the rest of the class, consider adding to the fun by having them vote on "alien awards" such as "Least Likely to Be Mistaken for Human" or "Most Out of This World."

Materials needed:
Reproducible student sheet on page 14 of this book; writing utensils

Materials needed:
Newsprint; Bibles; foil; tape; markers; make-up; other miscellaneous costume items

forgive you and guide you through life, you belong to this group of aliens! Today we're beginning a new study of the book of Ephesians. In that book, the apostle Paul talks a lot about these aliens we call Christians. In the coming weeks, we'll learn how Jesus has transformed us into his image, and we'll discover how that 'alien transformation' can revolutionize our lives and the world around us. Let's begin by taking a closer look at just what sort of aliens we've become."

MY FAVORITE ALIEN

Once everyone arrives, have students form pairs. Distribute writing utensils and copies of the reproducible student sheet titled "My Favorite Alien." Give students sufficient time to complete the sheet on their own, then have them share what they wrote with their partner. When pairs finish, gather everyone together and ask:

- **Why does it seem weird to think of yourself as an alien?**
- **How many of you would choose to take on alien characteristics if you could? Why or why not?**
- **How might life be easier for you if you had some of these alien qualities?**
- **How might life be more difficult for you if you had some of these alien qualities?**
- **How is being a Christian in the real world like being an alien?**

Conclude by saying, **"According to the Bible, there really is alien life on earth. The aliens are called Christians, and if you have a personal relationship with Jesus, you're one of them! This week we're beginning a new study of the book of Ephesians, in which the apostle Paul tells us a lot about what it means to be transformed into an 'alien' by the power of God. We'll see why being an 'alien' in Christ beats living as an ordinary human 'hands down.' Let's begin our exploration by taking a creative look at just what sort of alien life form we've become."**

Close Encounters

TRUE ALIEN TRANSFORMATIONS

Form groups of five or fewer. (If you chose to open the lesson with "Alien Transformations," you can just have students remain in their groups.) Set out the supplies and have each group choose a team captain. Have teams read together Ephesians 1:1-23. As they read, ask them to look for unique characteristics that describe what our new "alien" identity in Christ looks like.

Once teams have read the passage once or twice, instruct the team members to use the supplies you've provided to transform their team captain into an alien—based on the description in Ephesians 1:1-23. For example, students might wrap their team captain in newsprint to illustrate how Christians are "sealed" with the Holy Spirit (Ephesians 1:13), or they might tape a pair of eyes to his chest to illustrate how Christians have "eyes" in their heart (Ephesians 1:18). Encourage them to make the transformations as wild as possible.

If they are slow in getting started, here are a few more descriptions that might help:

- *holy in his sight* (v. 4)
- *adopted into his family* (v. 5)
- *riches lavished on us* (vv. 7, 8)

When teams are finished, let them present their team's "Christian" alien and explain his or her attributes to the rest of the group. Congratulate the teams on their creative work, then have the "aliens" remove their costumes. Read aloud Ephesians 1:4, 5, then say, **"It may seem odd for Christians to think of themselves as aliens among humans, but our adoption into God's family has not only allowed us to go to Heaven when we die—it's also transformed who we are right now. We are new creatures in Christ."**

I'M AN ALIEN?

Have students remain in their teams. Distribute copies of the reproducible student sheet on page 15. Then instruct them to discuss the questions on the sheet within their groups.

When groups are finished, have each student find a partner from another group and tell him or her one new insight he gleaned from reading Ephesians 1:1-23. Then gather everyone together and say, **"God has transformed us from ordinary people into an extraordinary 'alien' race who are members of God's family. And he accomplished all this through his Son, Jesus—who came to earth and died for our sins because he loves us and wants us to share in his supernatural life."**

METEOR MISHAP

Gather all the students together. If you haven't already done so, have them take turns reading different verses from Ephesians 1:1-23. Then ask for four or five volunteers to come to the front of your meeting room. Set out the stone and ask the volunteers to act out the following true story as you read it aloud:

"After a meteorite crashed into a village in Thailand's Petchabun province, local residents erected an altar nearby and began to gather at the site to pray for good luck. Many began to purchase lottery tickets, using numbers that they said they could see on the meteorite. The governor of the province then ordered the 37-pound meteorite seized, claiming that objects falling from the sky are the property of the government. Armed police guards had to be assigned to protect it after villagers began marching in protest to have the rock returned."[1]

After reading the story, thank the volunteers for their creativity in recreating the story. Then discuss these questions:

Check This . . .

As you begin this study of Ephesians, it may be helpful to give students a brief overview of the text. For example, the first half of Ephesians lists the Christian's heavenly possessions—such as adoption, redemption, inheritance, power, life, citizenship and the love of Christ. There are no commands listed in the first three chapters.

However, chapters four through six contain several commands, all of which focus on the Christian's responsibility to live out the Christian life in ways that are honoring to God. For example, Christians are to stop living the way they once did (4:22) and start living as a new person (4:24). We're also instructed to walk in holiness, treat others with love and respect and constantly prepare ourselves for spiritual warfare.

Materials needed:
Bibles; reproducible student sheet on page 15 of this book; writing utensils

Materials needed:
A stone; Bibles

- What do you think of the people who saw the meteorite as a "sign" from above?
- Why do you think people wanted to believe the meteorite had some kind of supernatural powers?
- Based on what you read in Ephesians 1:1-23, what would you say to the people who worshiped the meteorite?
- What are some ways we might act like the people in this story?
- How does this passage in Ephesians provide an answer for what the people in this story were looking for?
- How does this passage provide what we're looking for in our own lives?
- Which is easier to believe: a meteorite has the ability to tell you how to live or that God sent Jesus to show us who we are in Christ?
- What keeps you from believing that God has transformed you into a new creation in Christ?

Conclude by saying, **"Even though this was a true story, it's hard to believe it really happened. In the same way, even though everything we read in Ephesians 1 is true, it can be hard for us to believe sometimes, especially when we don't 'feel' transformed by God's power, and we still struggle with the same problems we had before we became Christians. But if we put our faith in God's Word, we will begin to see God's transforming power work in our lives—and we'll be changed forever."**

Life Invasion

ALIEN CONFIRMATION

Have students form pairs. Then say, **"All of us who have believed in Jesus have been transformed by God's power. We're no longer just human; we're also a part of God's family. And we have God's nature planted within us by the Holy Spirit. Even if you're unaware of it, there are probably ways in which you have already begun to be transformed to be like Jesus. Let's close our meeting by sharing some of those Christlike qualities that we see in each other."**

Have kids scan through Ephesians 1:1-23, then tell their partners one positive "alien" quality they see in one another. For example, someone might say, "You approach life with wisdom that I think comes from God," or "I appreciate the way you show God's love by always being willing to listen to others."

When pairs finish, close with the following prayer, based on Ephesians 1:17-19: **"God, I ask that you would give us the spirit of wisdom and revelation, so that we could know you better. I pray that the eyes of our hearts may be enlightened, so that we can know the hope you've called us to, receive the riches of your**

Materials needed:
Bibles

glorious inheritance and understand the incomparably great power you offer to those who believe in you. In the name of the one who started the invasion, amen."

REFLECTING ON THE LESSON

Form pairs and have partners take turns telling each other the way they would complete these sentences:

- **One important thing I've learned from this lesson is . . .**
- **One thing I'll do this week to help me apply what I've learned today is . . .**

If you have time, encourage students to tell the whole group how they completed the previous sentences. Then distribute copies of the reproducible student sheet titled "Alien Invasion Challenge" that's found on page 16 of this book. Conclude by saying, **"This week, let God invade your life by taking the challenge written on your sheet. Then tell us all about it next week."**

Close with the prayer written in the previous activity.

Materials needed:
Reproducible student sheet on page 16 of this book

1. In all the sci-fi movies and TV shows you've seen over the years, who or what is your favorite "alien" character?

2. What special attributes or abilities does your favorite alien possess?

3. Do you wish you had any of your alien's special abilities? Why or why not?

4. How would you respond if somebody told you that you actually were an alien—that you weren't like ordinary humans? Explain.

5. What evidence would you have to see to be convinced that you were something more than human?

6. Let's say someone recently convinced you that you were an alien. What sorts of questions about yourself would you like to have answered?

I'm an Alien?

Follow these instructions and discuss these questions in your group:

Read Ephesians 1:3-6.
- In this passage, Paul says that we've been blessed with *every* spiritual blessing in Christ. What do you think that means for you personally?

- Does knowing that you've been adopted as a child of God affect the way you see yourself? Why or why not?

Read Ephesians 1:7-14.
- What one thing stands out to you in this passage?

- Through our "adoption" into Christ's family, we've been redeemed, forgiven, chosen and sealed with the Holy Spirit. According to *Vine's Expository Dictionary of Biblical Words*, here's a quick overview of what those words mean:
  Redeemed—to be released from captivity, as the result of a ransom being paid.
  Forgiven—to be released from sin.
  Chosen—to have picked out something just for you.
  Sealed—to be sealed in a way that is secure and permanent.

- How might these words describe a process of transformation from being an ordinary person to being a child of God?

- According to Ephesians 1:13, what part did you play in this transformation?

Read Ephesians 1:15-23.
- Based on all you've read so far, why do you think it was important for Paul to pray for "the eyes of your heart" to be opened?

- Do you think the eyes of *your* heart have been opened in the way Paul describes? Why or why not?

- What's one way you want God to "open your eyes" through this study of Ephesians?

Before rejoining the group, pray briefly together, asking God to answer the prayer written in Ephesians 1:17-19 in your own lives.

ALIEN INVASION CHALLENGE

Every day this week, read and pray that God will answer Paul's prayer in Ephesians 1:17-19 in your own life. Then, each day, choose one way you can pursue knowing God better—and do it. For example, you might choose to interview your Christian friends about how they relate to God, or you might do a different "random act of kindness" for someone every day. Then think about how those actions help you become more like Jesus. At the end of the week, write in the space below your answer to these questions:

• How have "the eyes of my heart" been opened this week?

• Based on my experiences this past week, how would my life be different if I totally believed that God has adopted me as his child and given me a great inheritance by forgiving me and giving me his Holy Spirit?

A NEW RACE IN CHRIST

In this session, your students will create two three-dimensional murals—one that shows how God used to see them before they became Christians, and another that depicts how God views them now. By comparing these two murals, your group can understand how putting their faith in Christ did far more than ensure them a place in Heaven—it transformed them into a type of being that's radically different from who they used to be.

Sightings

1. MINOR TRANSFORMATIONS

Have students stand in a circle and closely look at each other. Encourage them to take note of what people are wearing and how they've arranged their clothing. Then ask them to turn and take one or two steps away from the circle—then secretly change one thing about their appearance. For example, they might unbutton a pocket, remove their earrings or untuck their shirt. The less noticeable the change, the better. When everyone is ready, have students turn back around and return to the circle. On "go," let them race to identify the changes other group members have made. Continue until every person's change has been identified.

While students remain in the circle, have them discuss these questions:

- **Was it difficult to identify some of the changes people made? Why or why not?**
- **How is the way we tried to hide these changes like the way people sometimes try to hide their Christianity from others?**
- **Why do we sometimes try to hide our Christian faith?**
- **What do you think might happen to our lives if we never tried to hide our Christianity from others?**

Conclude by saying, **"When we put our trust in Jesus and join God's family, a radical transformation takes place in our lives. Today we're going to explore exactly what happened to us when we became Christians, and discuss how that transformation can impact the way we live forever."**

LESSON TEXT
Ephesians 2:1-22

LESSON FOCUS
Jesus calls us to be a new race for his glory.

LESSON GOALS
As a result of participating in this lesson, students will:
- Explore what life was like before Jesus changed them.
- Experience how God created a whole new race in Christ.
- Discuss their reaction to being part of a new race of beings.

Materials needed:
Newsprint; foil; tape; markers; makeup; other miscellaneous costume items

Check This . . .
If students took the "Alien Invasion Challenge" last week, take a few minutes at the start of the lesson to let them share their experiences with the group.

TIME TRANSFORMATIONS

Give each person a piece of scratch paper and a pen. On their papers, have students write a brief description of one major "personality transformation" they've gone through in the past 10 years. For example, they might write that they used to be quiet and shy, but now they're much more outgoing. Have them fold their papers and drop them in a basket (or something similar). Then say, **"Now we'll test how well we know each other."** Read aloud each paper and let students guess who wrote it. If they can't guess correctly, have the person identify himself or herself. Then have students discuss these questions:

- **Do you think other people usually notice the personality changes you've experienced over the years? Why or why not?**
- **Do you think most people notice the changes you've experienced since becoming a Christian? Why or why not?**
- **Would you say becoming a Christian has transformed your life? Why or why not?**

Conclude by saying, **"When we become Christians, an incredible transformation takes place in our lives. We literally become totally new creatures. Unfortunately, lots of Christians don't realize what happened to them when they became Christians, so they continue living just like they always have. Today we're going to take a closer look at the transformation we experience when we choose to follow Jesus, and examine how that transformation can impact the way we live every day."**

Close Encounters

THE TRANSFORMATION WALL

Form two teams, and assign each team a different wall in your meeting room. (If you have more than 25 students, form four teams instead of two.) Name one team the "Before" group, and the other the "After" group.

Set out the supplies and have teams cover their designated area with newsprint. Then have the "Before" group read Ephesians 2:1-3, 11, 12; the "After" group should read Ephesians 2:4-10, 13-22. Comment, **"In a moment, you're going to transform your wall into a visual representation of what you just read in Scripture. Using the supplies I've provided (and anything you can find in the room), you're going to work with your team to create symbols and pictures that show what we were like before we became Christians, and what we're like now that we are Christians. When you're finished, we'll compare the two to see what discoveries we can make. This handout will help guide you."**

Give each person in the "Before" group a copy of page 22 of this book. Give each person in the "After" group a copy of page 23.

Allow students about 15 minutes to create their walls. Be available to help them come up with ideas for symbols or pictures to illustrate the truths they find in the passage. When they have completed their work, have a representative from each team read their assigned passage, then let another student explain their Transformation Wall creations. Then, have them discuss these questions within their teams:

- **What stands out most about what we've discovered so far?**
- **Which Transformation Wall best describes the way you see yourself right now? Explain.**
- **Does anything we've read seem hard for you to believe? Why or why not?**

Conclude by saying, **"This transformation from 'the way we were' to 'the way we are' can seem too good to be true, especially when we may not see the evidence of such a radical change in our daily lives right away. But these changes are real, and God is ready to make these changes in your life. Let's find out how."**

GOD'S WORKMANSHIP

Ask for two or three volunteers to come to the front of the room. Rip down a piece of "The Way We Were" Transformation Wall (any piece will do) and give it to the volunteers. Then say, **"I'll give you one minute to reshape this piece of 'The Way We Were' Transformation Wall to create an exact replica of any part of 'The Way We Are' Transformation Wall. Do your best, but remember, it has to be an exact duplication. Ready? Go!"**

Encourage the group to call out ideas. After one minute, examine their work. Regardless of how close they came to matching some symbol or drawing on "The Way We Are" transformation, they will not be able to match it exactly. Point out the flaws in their re-creation, then congratulate them for their efforts.

Next, have students form pairs to discuss these questions:

- **Why were our volunteers unsuccessful in their attempt?**
- **How is trying to re-create "The Way We Are" wall using "The Way We Were" materials like trying to transform our lives without God's help?**

Read aloud Ephesians 2:10. Then say, **"Since we are 'God's workmanship,' we have to rely on his power to transform our lives from being 'what we were' into 'what we are.' All that's required of us is to do our best to believe his Word and trust God to make this transformation real in our lives."**

Have pairs look again at "The Way We Are" Transformation Wall, then discuss these questions:

- **Do you think this Transformation Wall describes the way you see yourself? Why or why not?**
- **Based on what we've studied, do you think this Transformation Wall describes the way God sees you? Why or why not?**
- **What's one thing you can begin doing this week to change your thinking so that you begin to see yourself the same way God sees you?**

Check This . . .
As students create the Transformation Wall, play some music to motivate them as they work. One good song you could play is "This World," by Caedmon's Call. It can be found on their self-titled album.

Check This . . .
If you don't have sufficient wall space, just have kids use an open space on the floor instead.

Materials needed:
Bibles; Transformation Walls

Check This . . .
In Ephesians 2:13-20, Paul is specifically addressing the Gentile Christians who lived in Ephesus. According to ancient Jewish beliefs, non-Jews could not participate in the Jewish covenant with God unless they first became circumcised and obeyed the Jewish law. In this passage, Paul is emphasizing the point that the non-Jewish believers in Ephesus were entitled to the full benefits of the New Covenant with God—simply because they believed in Jesus. Because of their faith, they did not need to feel excluded from the Jewish heritage or think that they had to become a Jew in order to be a Christian.

Conclude by saying, **"When we become Christians, a lot of things change. We actually become totally new creations in Christ. But for us to experience that transformation in our daily lives, we have to choose to believe in what God has done, and change the way we see ourselves to match the way God now sees us. When that happens, the transformation that has already happened on the *inside* will begin to reveal itself on the *outside*."**

Materials needed:
Bibles

THE TRANSFORMING LOOK

Have students form a circle and take turns reading aloud Ephesians 2. Then ask:

- **How does it feel to hear how radically God has transformed our lives?**
- **Why do you think it's sometimes hard to believe we've really been changed?**
- **What would it take for you to totally believe what this passage tells us?**

Have students listen as you read this story about a man whose life was transformed:

"When I was in college, I was part of a fraternity initiation committee. We placed the new members in the middle of a long stretch of a country road. I was to drive my car as fast as possible straight at them. The challenge was for them to stand firm until a signal was given to jump out of the way. It was a dark night. I had reached 100 miles an hour and saw their looks of terror in the headlights. The signal was given and everyone jumped clear—except one boy. I left college after that. I later married and have two children.

"The look on that boy's face as I passed over him at 100 miles an hour stayed in my mind all the time. I became hopelessly inconsistent, moody and finally became a problem drinker. My wife had to work to bring in the only income we had. I was drinking at home one morning when someone rang the doorbell. I opened to find myself facing a woman who seemed strangely familiar. She sat down in our living room and told me she was the mother of the boy I had killed years before. She said that she had hated me and spent agonizing nights rehearsing ways to get revenge. I then listened as she told me of the love and forgiveness that had come when she gave her heart to Christ. She said, 'I have come to let you know that I forgive you and I want you to forgive me.' I looked into her eyes that morning and I saw deep in her eyes the permission to be the kind of man I might have been had I never killed that boy. That forgiveness changed my whole life."[1]

Have students form pairs to discuss these questions:

- **What's your reaction to this story?**
- **What caused the final transformation in the man's life?**
- **How does accepting someone's forgiveness change you?**
- **How can accepting God's forgiveness in our lives change us?**
- **How can this story help us understand how God can transform**

our lives the way Ephesians 2 describes?

Conclude, **"Receiving God's forgiveness in our lives changes us, just like receiving the mother's forgiveness changed the man in our story. As we learn to trust in God's forgiveness, we can begin to believe how forgiveness can transform our lives, and change us from what we once were into something totally new and miraculous."**

Life Invasion

THE TRANSFORMING POWER OF FORGIVENESS

Have students form trios, and have them read aloud Ephesians 2:3-7. Then say, **"God transformed our lives when we received Christ's forgiveness for our sins. But even though God has forgiven us, that doesn't mean we stop sinning altogether, or that we no longer need his forgiveness in our daily lives. Let's close today by thanking God for the ongoing power of his forgiveness at work in our lives."**

Give each person a long strip of ribbon and a marker. Instruct each person to think of the one sin he or she struggles with most. Then have each student draw a symbol to represent that sin on his or her ribbon. When they finish, have trio members help each person bind his or her wrists together with the ribbon. Then say, **"Now give your trio members a big hug!"** After students struggle to hug each other, have them discuss this question in their groups:

- **How does daily sin keep us from loving others the way God has called us to love?**

Set out several pairs of scissors, and allow trios to free each other from their bonds. Then have them discuss, **"How does forgiveness free us to love others the way God wants?"**

Close by saying, **"Now give each other a big hug—this time for real!"**

REFLECTING ON THE LESSON

Form pairs, and have partners take turns telling each other the way they would complete these sentences:

- **One important thing I've learned from this lesson is . . .**
- **One thing I'll do this week to help me apply what I've learned today is . . .**

If you have time, encourage students to tell the whole group how they completed the previous sentences. Then distribute copies of the reproducible student sheet titled "Alien Invasion Challenge" that's found on page 24 of this book. Conclude by saying, **"This week, let God invade your life by taking the challenge written on your sheet. Then tell us all about it next week."**

Close with prayer.

Materials needed:
Bibles; ribbons; markers; scissors

Materials needed:
Reproducible sheet on page 24 of this book

The Way We Were

In your team, read together Ephesians 2:1-3, 11, 12. Based on the passage, brainstorm together some characteristics that describe the way we *were* before we became Christians. Here are a few examples to get you started:

• We were dead because we were sinful (2:1).
• We used to follow Satan and the evil ways of this world (2:2).
• We used to serve our sinful nature, gratifying its cravings, desires and thoughts (2:3).

• _____
• _____
• _____
• _____
• _____

For each of the characteristics you've listed above, think of a symbol or picture that can illustrate that characteristic. Here are a few examples to get you started:

• "We were dead . . ." — You could make a tombstone out of newsprint, or draw a skull and crossbones.
• "We used to follow Satan . . . " — You could make a three-dimensional "broken heart" out of newsprint, or draw stick figures of people walking into a pit.

• _____
• _____
• _____
• _____
• _____
• _____

Now, work together to create the symbols or drawings you've come up with on the Transformation Wall.
Across the top of the newsprint, write "The Way We Were."

The Way We Are

In your team, read together Ephesians 2:4-10, 13-22. Based on the passage, brainstorm together some characteristics that describe the way God has transformed us now that we're Christians. Here are a few examples to get you started:

- We are now alive from the dead (2:5).
- We are now seated with Christ in the heavenly realms (2:6).
- We have become God's "works of art," created in Christ to do good works (2:10).

- _____
- _____
- _____
- _____
- _____

For each of the characteristics you've listed above, think of a symbol or picture that can illustrate that characteristic. Here are a few examples to get you started:

- "We are alive from the dead . . ." — You could show people walking out of a tomb.
- "We are seated with Christ . . ." — You could decorate a chair to make it look like a throne, place it against the Transformation Wall, then show one of your group members sitting in it.

- _____
- _____
- _____
- _____
- _____
- _____

Now, work together to create the symbols or drawings you've come up with on the Transformation Wall. Across the top of the newsprint, write "The Way We Are."

ALIEN INVASION CHALLENGE

Sometime early this week, write a one-paragraph description of how God sees you, based on Ephesians 2:4-10, 13-22. Then share your thoughts with a friend, asking him or her to pray that you would begin to see yourself the way God sees you.

Then, at the end of the week, write responses to these questions:

• How did I change my perspective this week on how I see myself?

• Based on the description I wrote this week, how would my life be different if I totally believed in the teachings found in Ephesians 2 for the rest of my life?

THE PRIME DIRECTIVE

In this session, students will create a visual representation of the love they have for someone they care deeply about and compare their creation to Jesus, whom God sent as a representation of his love for us. Through this exploration, students can realize that the power of God's love is stronger than any force in the universe, and that it's through his love that they are changed and empowered to love others.

The phrase "Prime Directive" originates from the monumentally-popular series *Star Trek*. In the show (and all its spin-offs), the Prime Directive is the first rule of space exploration. It states, in essence, that "we shall never in any way interfere with the natural development of any other intelligent life form." In the years since the show began, this fictional rule has developed into one of the philosophical tenets of popular culture. In current lingo, it might be phrased more like: "That's your space; this is my space. Stay out of my space."

That's quite different from the "Prime Directive" Paul endorses for Christians in the book of Ephesians. In fact, Paul encourages Christians to "invade" other people's lives with demonstrations of God's love. That's a far cry from the notion of "noninvolvement" supported by the producers of *Star Trek*.

LESSON TEXT
Ephesians 3:1-21

LESSON FOCUS
Jesus empowers us through his Spirit to make a difference in our world.

LESSON GOALS
As a result of participating in this lesson, students will:
- Unravel the secret mystery of the gospel.
- Discover the "Prime Directive" for all Christians.
- Challenge each other to follow the "Prime Directive" no matter what.

Sightings

1 TOWER OF POWER

Form four teams and assign each team a different corner of the room. Set out a stack of assorted magazines, tape and scissors. Then point to the chairs and say, **"Work with your team to stack two or three of these chairs in your corner so that you create a tower. Then, using pictures and words from these magazines, create a 'tower of power'—that is, cover your tower with words or images that illustrate what you consider to be real power."**

Allow teams five minutes to complete their towers. When time is up, let each group explain its creation to the rest of the students. Then have them discuss this question in their teams: **"Based on all you see here, what do you think is the greatest form of power in the world? Explain."**

Check This . . .
If students took the "Alien Invasion Challenge" last week, take a few minutes at the start of the session to have them share their experiences with the group.

Materials needed:
Chairs or tables; assorted popular magazines; masking tape; scissors

Check This . . .
If the chairs or tables in your classroom don't stack well, have kids just create their "tower" on the meeting room wall.

Conclude by saying, **"Today we're going to examine a power that is greater than technology, money, fame or position. It's a unique power that God has given to all his children—in fact, it's the one ability that makes Christians stand out as 'aliens' in this world. Let's take a look at why it's so important and how we can use it."**

ALIEN ABILITIES

Gather students in a huddle in the center of the room. Then say, **"We've all seen movies or TV shows where an alien being had some awesome or mysterious powers that we humans don't have. And if you're like most people, you've day-dreamed about what it might be like to have special powers. I'm going to name three special powers that different alien characters might have. Once I call them out, I'd like you to choose which one of the three special powers you most wish you had. Don't say your choice aloud just yet."**

Call out these three alien abilities:
- the ability to read minds
- the ability to fly
- the ability to be impervious to injury

Have students quietly decide which one they would most like to have. Then have them move to different parts of the room depending on the choice they made. For example, have those who'd like the ability to read minds move to one corner of the room, those who'd like to fly move to the opposite corner and the third group stay in the center of the room.

Ask several volunteers from each group to explain why they chose that particular alien ability over the others. Then say, **"I've got some startling news for you. As Christians, we live as 'aliens' in this world. And God has given us a special alien ability that is more powerful by far than any of the powers I've just named. Today we're going to examine what that special power is, and how we can use it to help others."**

Close Encounters

LOVE BUBBLES

Gather everyone in a circle, then set out the supplies in the center of the room. Give each person a balloon. Have students inflate their balloons and tie them off. Tell them each to think of someone they care for deeply such as a parent, a friend or a significant other. Then have kids use their balloons as a "canvas" for creating a visual representation of the love they feel for that significant person in their lives. For example, they can cut out images from the magazines that illustrate their love, then tape those images to the balloon. Or they might use the markers to draw symbols or words that describe the love they feel for their special person.

When they have finished their "love bubbles," have them form pairs and share with their partner who their special person is and the meaning behind the various images and symbols they collected. Then ask partners to discuss these questions with one another:

- **Was it hard or easy to create your "love bubble"? Why?**
- **Was it hard or easy to talk about your creation with someone else? Explain.**
- **If you gave your creation to the special person you made it for, how do you think he or she would respond? Explain.**
- **How would you respond if that significant person in your life took your creation and destroyed it?**

Conclude by saying, **"I'm sure none of the special people in our lives would purposefully destroy something we made for them. But that *did* happen to God, when he sent his Son, Jesus, to earth as a gift of love from his heart. People killed Jesus. Nevertheless, he still brought us a gift that makes us more powerful than any force in the universe. You're holding representations of that gift in your hands right now. Let's look more closely at this awesome 'special power' that God gave us in Christ."**

THE MYSTERIOUS POWER OF LOVE

Form groups of five or fewer and give each group a balloon. Have them read Ephesians 3:1-12. Using the same supplies as in the previous activity, ask group members to work together to create a "love bubble" that represents the love God showed us through Christ—based on the verses they just read. As before, students can use magazine images that they cut out and tape to the balloon, or they can draw symbols or write words using the permanent markers.

Materials needed:
Bibles; balloons; magazines; permanent markers; tape; scissors; blank paper; writing utensils

When all groups have completed their work, have them each explain their creation to all the students. Then have groups each destroy their Jesus "love bubble" creations. When all the creations have been destroyed, have groups discuss these questions:

- **How did it feel to destroy your Jesus "love bubble" creation?**
- **How is that like what happened to Jesus in real life?**
- **Did Jesus' death mean that he failed to bring God's salvation to us? Why or why not?**
- **How did his death actually demonstrate God's all-powerful love for us?**
- **How can that "special power" of love have an effect on our lives today?**

After the discussion, have groups read Ephesians 3:13-21. Give each group scratch paper and writing utensils and have them rewrite the passage into a prayer that they can pray for each other right now. As groups finish doing this, have them kneel in a circle and pray for one another.

After all groups have prayed, conclude, **"Because we're Christians, others may see us as aliens in this world, just like** they saw Jesus as a sort of 'alien' who didn't fit into their way of life. But because of what Jesus has done for us, we've been given a 'special power' of love that is stronger than any weapon forged against us in this world. God's love conquers all."

③ THE POWER OF LOVE

Have students form groups of five or fewer, possibly by choosing their favorite Olympic sport. (Give them five sports from which to choose and have them go to designated areas of the room if they like swimming, gymnastics, basketball, skating, etc.) Give each group a copy of the reproducible student sheet found on page 30 of this book. Have groups read the quotes and the assigned Bible verses, then discuss the questions at the bottom of the sheet.

When they finish, conclude by saying, **"Emmet Fox once wrote that 'if only you could love enough, you would be the happiest and most powerful being in the world.' Jesus loved more than any person in history. And his love now resides in the hearts of all those who have trusted him with their lives. That makes us very powerful people in this world. We can change people's lives with the power of Christ's love within us. In fact, showing God's love to others is the primary reason we're here."**

Materials needed:
Bibles; reproducible student sheet on page 30 of this book

Life Invasion

① OUR PRIME DIRECTIVE

Have students stay in their groups of five. Give each group a pen and a copy of the reproducible student sheet on page 31 of this book. Ask groups to follow the instructions on the sheet for creating a "Prime Directive" based on Paul's prayer in Ephesians 3.

When groups finish, have them each read their "Prime Directive" and explain how they came up with it. Tape a sheet of butcher paper to the wall, and have groups work together to merge their "Prime Directives" into one final version that everyone likes. Conclude by saying, **"Write this 'Prime Directive' in your Bible, and memorize it. Then you can think of it every day as go to school or work or spend time with friends. Let it motivate you to use your 'special power' of love to powerfully impact the world around you for Jesus."**

Close with prayer.

Materials needed:
Reproducible student sheet on page 31 of this book; Bibles; writing utensils; butcher paper; masking tape; magic marker

REFLECTING ON THE LESSON

Form pairs, and have partners take turns telling each other the way they would complete these sentences:

- **One important thing I've learned from this lesson is . . .**
- **One thing I'll do this week to help me apply what I've learned today is . . .**

If you have time, encourage students to tell the whole group how they completed the previous sentences. Then distribute copies of the reproducible student sheet titled "Alien Invasion Challenge" that's found on page 32 of this book. Conclude by saying, **"This week, let God invade your life by taking the challenge written on your sheet. Then tell us all about it next week."**

Close with prayer.

Materials needed:
Reproducible student sheet on page 32 of this book

The POWER of Love

Read the following quotes and Bible verses, then discuss the questions below with your group members.

"Of all powers, love is the most powerful and the most powerless. It is the most powerful because it alone can conquer that final and most impregnable stronghold which is the human heart. It is the most powerless because it can do nothing except by consent."

—Frederick Buechner

"Love is the most durable power in the world. This creative force is the most potent instrument available in mankind's quest for peace and security."—Martin Luther King, Jr.

"Love conquers all; and we must yield to love."—Virgil

"Love is the strongest force the world possesses, and yet it is the humblest imaginable."
—Mohandas K. Gandhi

"One cannot be strong without love. For love is not an irrelevant emotion; it is the blood of life, the power of reunion of the separated."—Paul Tillich

"Place me like a seal over your heart, like a seal on your arm; for love is as strong as death, its jealousy unyielding as the grave. It burns like blazing fire, like a mighty flame. Many waters cannot quench love; rivers cannot wash it away. If one were to give all the wealth of his house for love, it would be utterly scorned."
—Song of Songs 8:6, 7

Read Ephesians 3:16-21. Then discuss these questions:
- **Why is love so powerful?**
- **How can God's love for us help us love others powerfully?**
- **Why is it sometimes hard to believe in God's love for us?**
- **How can we help each other love better?**
- **Why do you think it's important for Christians to love others powerfully?**

The Christian PRIME DIRECTIVE

In your group, read aloud Ephesians 3:16-21. Based on these verses, create a statement that describes our primary purpose as Christians who want to follow Jesus. Write that "Prime Directive" in the space below:

ALIEN INVASION CHALLENGE

Every day this week, take time to pray for yourself using Paul's prayer in Ephesians 3:14-21 as a guide. Then, at some point during the week, rewrite the prayer in 3:14-21 to create a personal "Prime Directive" for your life. For example, you might simply list three or four things you think God wants you to do with your life based on this Scripture. Once you create your personal "Prime Directive," memorize it and use it to encourage you to love others better, and to follow God's will for your life.

At the end of the week, write responses to the questions below:

• How did I follow God's "Prime Directive" for my life this week?

• Based on my experiences this week, how would my life be different if I lived according to my personal "Prime Directive" for the rest of my life?

ONE ALIEN NATION (UNDER GOD)

4

In this session, students will participate in several different activities that demonstrate what Christian unity is all about. Then they will design their own model of unity based on the teachings of Ephesians 4. Through this study, they will see that Christian unity is uniquely different and better than other kinds of unity they might find in the world, and they'll learn how they can build Christian unity in practical ways in the coming weeks.

Sightings

ONE-HANDED KNOTS

Have students form a circle. While holding one hand behind their backs, have them attempt to untie and retie one of their shoes. (If some students don't have laces on their shoes, have them borrow a shoe from someone who does.) After a few minutes, stop the action and ask:

- **Why are you having so much trouble doing such a simple task?**

Have students use both hands to retie their shoes, then ask:

- **Why was it so much easier that time?**
- **How is the way your hands work together similar to the way people work together to accomplish tasks in real life?**
- **How is trying to tie your shoe with one hand like trying to be a lone ranger?**
- **Do you think cooperation and unity with others is important in your life? Why or why not?**
- **Do you think cooperation and unity with others is important in the church? Why or why not?**

Conclude by saying, **"Because we're Christians, God has called us to be different from the people of the world. But he's also called us to stand united with other Christians and work together to accomplish his will. Today we're going to explore why unity among Christians is so important to God—and so difficult for us."**

LESSON TEXT
Ephesians 4:1-32

LESSON FOCUS
Jesus unites all believers under his lordship.

LESSON GOALS
As a result of participating in this lesson, students will:

- Discover why unity in Christ is so important.
- Explore how to pursue unity with others.
- Learn what will happen when unity is achieved.

Materials needed:
Shoes with laces

Check This . . .
If students took the "Alien Invasion Challenge" last week, take a few minutes at the start of the session to have them share their experiences with the group.

Check This . . .
A song that reflects this lesson well is "Unite," recorded by the Supertones on their release *Supertones Strike Back*.

Materials needed:
Reproducible student sheet on page 38 of this book; writing utensils

 ## WHAT IF . . . ?

Form five groups, perhaps by asking students their favorite kind of pizza (extra cheese, pepperoni, sausage, veggie and supreme). Give each group a pen and a copy of the reproducible student sheet on page 38 of this book. Assign each group a different section of the handout and have groups work together to write a response to their assigned question. When groups finish, have them each share their response with the rest of the students. Then ask:

- **Which of these models of unity do you think would work best for the church? Explain.**
- **Which models do you think would cause problems for Christians? Explain.**

Have a volunteer read aloud Ephesians 4:1-6, then ask:
- **Which of these models of unity does the Bible endorse?**
- **Why do you think the Bible endorses these models and not the others?**

Conclude by saying, **"As we're going to discover today, unity is very important to God. But that doesn't mean he wants us to be unified in the same way people of the world find unity. He wants us to be unified in a way that's uniquely Christian. Let's see how we can develop his kind of unity in our lives."**

Close Encounters

BIND US TOGETHER?

Materials needed:
Bibles; belts

Have everyone gather in the center of the room and remove their belts. (Be sure to bring several extra belts of your own, in case some aren't wearing belts.) Strap all the belts together in a chain, then wrap the belts around the huddled group and tighten the two ends together so that students are bound together snugly. Then ask the group to work together to perform a few simple tasks around the church. For example, ask them to collect the trash in several rooms and carry it out to the dumpster; ask them to go to the pastor, or someone similar, and say a prayer for him or her; ask them to arrange the classroom chairs into a circle to prepare for the next activity. After they've completed a few tasks, untie them and ask:

- **Do you think this was a good demonstration of Christian unity? Why or why not?**
- **What did you like about the kind of unity we just demonstrated?**
- **What did you *not* like about it?**

Comment, **"What we just did might demonstrate a kind of unity, but I'm not sure it's the kind of unity the Bible teaches that we should have. Let's see if you can find a better way to demonstrate real Christian unity."**

Form groups of six or fewer. Have groups read Ephesians 4:1-32. Based on those verses, have each group come up with a demonstration that they think best illustrates the kind of unity God wants Christians to have with one another. Tell groups their demonstration doesn't necessarily have to be like the one they just did. For example, instead of an activity, they might choose to sing a song, perform a skit or play a game that they create. Anything goes, as long as it demonstrates the kind of unity they see in the Bible passage.

When groups are ready, have them each present their demonstrations. After each presentation, lead students in discussing these questions:

- **How does this demonstration reflect the kind of unity God wants Christians to have?**
- **How is this kind of unity different from the kinds of "unity" you see promoted in the world around us?**

After all the demonstrations have been presented, say, **"Christian unity is very important to God. And it should be important to us, too. Without it, we would each be like 'lone ranger' aliens living alone in the world, and we wouldn't be able to accomplish God's will in the way he intended. Let's explore how we can develop this special kind of Christian unity with each other in some practical ways."**

IN PURSUIT OF UNITY

Have students remain in their same groups from the previous activity, and give each group newsprint, tape and markers. Have groups tape their newsprint to the wall, and open their Bibles to Ephesians 4. Then say, **"On 'go,' I want your group to race against the other groups in listing all the ways we can pursue true Christian unity with each other, based on the information in Ephesians 4. You can borrow ideas from other groups' lists all you want. The group with the longest list wins."**

Start the race. Allow groups three to five minutes to make their lists. Then call time and count the items to determine which list is the longest. After congratulating the winners, ask:

- **Was this race a good demonstration of the kind of unity God wants Christians to have? Why or why not?**
- **How could we have done this activity differently so that it would better demonstrate the kind of unity described in Ephesians 4?**
- **Of all the ways you've listed, which ones do you see happening regularly in our group? in the church at large?**
- **Which of the ways we've listed do you rarely see happening in our group? in the church at large?**

Conclude by saying, **"Because we're Christians, we should act differently from the rest of the world. We really need each other for support and encouragement as we work together to accomplish God's will in the world. I encourage you to think about how you can adopt one of the ideas we've come up with here and begin to practice it in your own life. We need to stick together and believe in each other. We're all part of the same family—and we're all members of Christ's body."**

Check This . . .
Many scholars believe that Paul wrote Ephesians for a wider audience than simply the Christians at Ephesus. The only reference to the Ephesians is found in 1:1. But the phrase "to the saints in Ephesus" is not found in the two oldest Greek manuscripts. That fact supports the idea that this epistle was likely a "circular letter" designed to be read by many congregations in Asia Minor. That also may explain why Paul focuses so heavily on the importance of unity in the body of Christ, even though the church at Ephesus was not known to suffer extensively from divisions in the church.

Materials needed:
Bibles; newsprint; masking tape; markers

Check This . . .
While students make their lists, play the song "People Like Me," by Audio Adrenaline. It can be found on their CD titled *Some Kind Of Zombie*.

Materials needed:
Bibles

3 WE ALL WIN TOGETHER

Read this true story to your group:

"Some missionaries in the Philippines set up a croquet game in their front yard. Several of their Agta Negrito neighbors became interested and wanted to join the fun. The missionaries explained the game and started them out, each with a mallet and ball. As the game progressed, opportunity came for one of the players to take advantage of another by knocking that person's ball out of the court. A missionary explained the procedure, but his advice only puzzled the Negrito friend.

'Why would I want to knock his ball out of the court?' he asked.

'So you will be the one to win!' a missionary said. The short-statured man shook his head in bewilderment. Competition is generally ruled out in a hunting and gathering society, where people survive not by competing but by sharing equally in every activity.

The game continued, but no one followed the missionaries' advice. When a player successfully got through all the wickets, the game was not over for him. He went back and gave aid and advice to his fellows. As the final player moved toward the last wicket, the affair was still very much a team effort. And finally, when the last wicket was played, the 'team' shouted happily, 'We won! We won!'

That is how the church, the body of Christ, should be. We're a team. We all win together."[1]

After reading the story, ask:

- **Do you agree with the message of this story? Why or why not?**
- **Why does the church often find it so hard to be unified?**
- **What makes it hard for you to feel united with other Christians?**
- **What do you do that makes it hard for other Christians to feel united with you?**

Have several volunteers take turns reading different verses from Ephesians 4:1-32. Then ask:

- **What does this passage say to you about unity?**
- **Based on this passage, what are some ways you can start building Christian unity in our group this week? in the church at large?**

Conclude by saying, "**Unless we walk in unity as Christians, we will all end up losers. That's because we were never designed to live as 'lone ranger' Christians. We need each other's love and support every day in order to fully obey God and follow his will for our lives.**"

Life Invasion

COMMITMENT TO UNITY

Form a circle, then say, **"I'm going to call out four words. As I mention each word, I'll point to a different section of the room. Once you've heard all four words, decide which word best represents your interests and move to the appropriate section of the room."**

Here are the words:
- school
- sports
- family
- music

Once students are in four groups, have them form smaller groups by narrowing their interests even more. For example, have the "school" group divide according to favorite classes. Have the "family" group divide according to favorite relationships within the family. Have the "sports" group divide according to favorite sport and have the "music" group divide according to favorite style of music.

Once everyone is divided up, say, **"There certainly are a lot of differences between us. But true unity can still happen because we have one thing in common—Jesus!"**

Have students return to the circle, then give each person a copy of the student sheet found on page 39 of this book. Based on what they read in Ephesians 4, have students work together to come up with three new ways the whole group can work together to build Christian unity in the group by focusing on Jesus. For example, they might agree never to use put-downs, they might decide to take their Bibles to school or agree to meet together to pray outside of church once a week. When they finish, have them write their three ideas on one of the handouts, and have each person sign it.

Conclude by saying, **"Christian unity is important to God. And it starts right here with us. Let's hold each other accountable to follow through with our commitments this week."**

Close with prayer.

REFLECTING ON THE LESSON

Form pairs, and have partners take turns telling each other the way they would complete these sentences:
- **One important thing I've learned from this lesson is . . .**
- **One thing I'll do this week to help me apply what I've learned today is . . .**

If you have time, encourage students to tell the whole group how they completed the previous sentences. Then distribute copies of the reproducible student sheet titled "Alien Invasion Challenge" that's found on page 40 of this book. Conclude by saying, **"This week, let God invade your life by taking the challenge written on your sheet. Then tell us all about it next week."**

Close with prayer.

Materials needed:
Reproducible student sheet on page 39 of this book; Bibles; writing utensils

Check This . . .
Encourage students to use the lists they created to help them come up with specific ideas for building unity in the group.

Materials needed:
Reproducible student sheet on page 40 of this book

What if Christians treated the church like a corporation . . .
how would you measure unity in a church like that?

Group 1

What if Christians treated the church like a social club . . .
how would you measure unity in a church like that?

Group 3

What if Christians treated the church like a military dictatorship . . .
how would you measure unity in a church like that?

Group 2

What if Christians treated the church like a living organism, a sort of "body" . . .
how would you measure unity in a church like that?

Group 5

What if Christians treated the church like a family . . .
how would you measure unity in a church like that?

Group 4

FIRST CHURCH OF FREEDOM

COmMItMEnT TO UnITy

"You were all called to travel on the same road and in the same direction, so stay together, both outwardly and inwardly." —Ephesians 4:3, from THE MESSAGE. Copyright © 1993. Used by permission of NavPress Publishing Group.

In the space below, write three new ways we can work together to begin to build unity in our group this week:

 1.

 2.

 3.

ALIEN INVASION CHALLENGE

After reading through Ephesians 4:1-32 a few more times, every day this week look for ways other Christians you know are helping to build unity in your group or in the church at large. For example, you might notice the way one of your friends takes time to listen to others, or you might observe a specific way your pastor works hard to build unity in your church. Then, at the end of the week, send a postcard to each person you noticed, thanking him or her for helping to build unity in the church and for inspiring you to build unity with other Christians too.

At the end of the week, write responses to the questions below:

• How did I help build unity in our group this week? in the church at large?

• Based on my experiences this week, how would my life be different if I made building Christian unity a priority for the rest of my life?

RESPECTING OTHER LIFE FORMS

In this session, students will form groups to examine specific ways God wants Christians to show love and respect to their families, co-workers and friends. Then they'll create instructional video clips to apply what they've learned to daily life. Through this experience, they can realize that God wants them to always show respect to others, regardless of how they act.

Sightings

1 MACHINE REPLICATORS

Form two equal groups. Tell groups that their goal is to work together to create a "human machine." To create their machine, all group members must be connected in some way—by leaning on each other, holding hands or something similar. And each person must have a "moving part"—by waving a hand or tapping a foot, for example. Explain that their machine doesn't have to do anything; it just has to look like a big human mechanism.

If possible, have one group move to a different room while students design their machines. Then, when groups are ready, have them come back together. Have one group demonstrate its machine for the other. Then challenge the second team to see how quickly it can duplicate the first team's machine. Once they've accomplished the feat (or at least come close), have teams switch roles to see which team can duplicate the other's machine the quickest.

After both have made the attempt, gather everyone together and read aloud Ephesians 5:1. Then ask:

- **What was hard about duplicating the other group's machine?**
- **How is this activity like trying to imitate Christ in the real world?**

Conclude by saying, **"Today we're going to explore how we can imitate Christ in four important areas: in our families, at our jobs, in our relationships with non-Christians and in our relationships with our Christian friends. Through this exploration we'll discover how important it is to always respect others, regardless of how they treat us."**

LESSON TEXT
Ephesians 5:1–6:9

LESSON FOCUS
Jesus helps us live a life of love for others.

LESSON GOALS
As a result of participating in this lesson, students will:
- Examine how aliens should treat their human friends.
- Explore how aliens should treat their families and co-workers.
- Discuss how they can use their alien influence to change the world.

Check This . . .
If students took the "Alien Invasion Challenge" last week, take a few minutes at the start of the session to have them share their experiences with the group.

Check This . . .
Two excellent songs that deal with today's lesson are "Declaration" and "Scattering." Both of them are recorded by Geoff Moore and the Distance on their *Threads* album.

Materials needed:
Reproducible student sheet on page 46 of this book; writing utensils

Check This . . .
The word translated "alien" in Ephesians is actually the Greek word *apallotrio*, which essentially means "to be a stranger to," "to be rendered an alien" or "to be alienated." In Ephesians, Paul refers to non-Christians as people who are "alien" to God and the new life he offers in Christ. But, as Paul explains, when we believe in the gospel, God transforms us so that we are "no longer foreigners and aliens" to God (Ephesians 2:19), but have become "aliens" to the world and its ways. Make sure students understand this distinction as they discuss reasons why we should become imitators of God and stop imitating the ways of the world.

Materials needed:
Bibles; paper; writing utensils

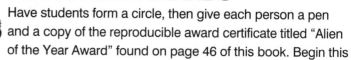

BEST ALIEN AWARDS

Have students form a circle, then give each person a pen and a copy of the reproducible award certificate titled "Alien of the Year Award" found on page 46 of this book. Begin this activity by saying, **"Think of the one person you think is the best example of what it means to live the Christian lifestyle. That person may be someone you know, or just someone you've read about or seen on television. Once you've decided on your person, write his or her name on the award certificate I just gave you."**

When students are finished, have them form pairs. Have them tell their partner who they chose as their "model Christian" and why. Then have pairs discuss these questions:

- **Why do you suppose the award calls your role model an "alien"?**
- **Do you think other people might see the person you chose as a sort of "alien" compared to most people? Why or why not?**
- **What qualities do you see in that person that you'd like to have in your own life?**
- **If you had those qualities, do you think other people might be less likely to understand you? Why or why not?**

Read aloud Ephesians 5:1. Then conclude by saying, **"We can all find examples of Christian men and women whom we would like to emulate. Ultimately, though, we should all look to God as our supreme example and try to emulate him. When we do, though, we shouldn't be surprised if other people fail to understand our lifestyle, or accept us for who we are.**

"Today we're going to explore how we should be imitators of God in the way we treat others—our families, our co-workers, our non-Christian friends and even other Christians. We'll see the importance of always respecting others, whether they understand us or not."

Close Encounters

GOOD IDEA/BAD IDEA

Form four groups, possibly by allowing students to choose their "most hated vegetable." Let students who choose asparagus gather in one part of the room, those who name spinach in another part, cauliflower a third place and beets a fourth place. After they have gathered in their groups, assign each of them one of these topics:

- Christian friends — Ephesians 5:1-21
- Non-Christian friends — Ephesians 5:1-21
- Families — Ephesians 5:22–6:4
- Co-Workers — Ephesians 6:5-9

Tell groups their goal is create a "Good Idea/Bad Idea" instructional video clip based on their assigned topic and Bible passage. Tell them to pretend their clip will be filmed and used in a future instructional class for new Christians.

To create their clip, have groups read their assigned passage, then draw from it one example of a "good idea" Christians should follow when dealing with their assigned people group, and one "bad idea" Christians should avoid when dealing with that same people group. For example, the "families" group might create a clip illustrating the "good idea" of children obeying their parents, and the "bad idea" of fathers "exasperating" their kids.

Once each group has come up with its two ideas, give them a little time to practice how they'll present their video clip to the class. Then let students discuss these questions in their groups:

- **What stands out to you about the Scripture we read?**
- **Why do you think it's so important for Christians to treat other people with respect?**
- **When do you struggle with treating friends, co-workers or family members with respect?**
- **How can God help you show respect in those times?**

Conclude the discussion by saying, **"Now let's see what you have created to help us learn how to live as Christians in the real world."**

HOW TO BE A GOOD ALIEN

When groups are ready, have them each read their assigned passage to the class, then takes turns showing their video clip to the rest of the group. To avoid any confusion, encourage groups to present their ideas in sequence—the "good idea" followed by the "bad idea." After each group presents its clip, congratulate students on their creativity and insight. Once all the clips have been presented, have students locate one person from each of the other groups to create a group of four. Then have foursomes discuss these questions:

- **How do you know when someone respects you?**
- **What can you do specifically to show respect to your non-Christian friends? your Christian friends? your family members? your co-workers?**
- **How is respecting others a way of imitating God?**
- **Why is respect important to you?**
- **Why do you think respect is important to God?**

Conclude by saying, **"Respect is important to God. That's why he's given us specific instructions on how Christians should treat the people in their lives. Someone once said that 'respect is love in plain clothes.' When we respect others, regardless of how they treat us, we demonstrate God's love in a way that can have an eternal impact on other people's lives."**

SAFE FROM LOVE

To begin this activity, ask students to form a circle and join hands. Have them close their eyes and lean back so that their weight is supported by holding onto their neighbors' hands. As they do so, read this quote from David Watson,

Check This . . .
If you have access to video equipment, consider actually filming your students' presentations, then watching them together at the end of the session, or showing them to another group within the church.

Materials needed:
Bibles

from his book, *I Believe in the Church*:

> **"To love all is to be vulnerable. Love anything, and your heart will certainly be wrung and possibly broken. If you want to make sure of keeping it intact, you must give your heart to no one. . . . Wrap it carefully round with hobbies and little luxuries; avoid all entanglements; lock it safe in a casket or coffin of your selfishness. But in that casket—safe, dark, motionless, airless—it will change. It will not be broken; it will become unbreakable, impenetrable, irredeemable. . . . The only place outside heaven where you can be perfectly safe from all the dangers of love is—hell."[1]**

After reading the quote, have students open their eyes and stand up straight. Then ask them to turn to a partner and discuss these questions:

- **How is the risk you took in leaning back like the risk involved in loving others boldly for Christ?**
- **Does the idea of getting your heart broken frighten you? Why or why not?**
- **How can God help us love and respect others, even when they don't treat us well?**

After the discussion, have pairs read Ephesians 5:1–6:9 together, looking for ways God can help them love and respect others regardless of how they're treated. Then have pairs pray together, asking God to help them show respect and love for others in a way that leads them closer to Jesus.

Life Invasion

1 IMITATE GOD

Have students return to their four groups from the Good Idea/Bad Idea activity. (If you didn't do that activity, just divide them into four groups.) Remind each group of its assigned people group—families, co-workers, Christian friends and non-Christian friends. Give each group a copy of the reproducible student sheet found on page 47 of this book. Have groups follow the instructions on the handout for their assigned people group.

When groups are finished, distribute scissors and have them cut apart their handout along the dotted lines. Gather all the strips from each group, shuffle them together, then redistribute them to the class, giving one strip at random to each person.

Close by saying, **"In your hand you hold a 'good idea' that you can carry out this week. I encourage you to take your strip home and, sometime this week, do what it says. Then come back next week and tell us how it went. Remember, respect is important to God. Do your best to show respect for others this week."**

Close with prayer.

Materials needed:
Reproducible student sheet on page 47 of this book; writing utensils; scissors

Check This . . .
While groups work on their sheets, play the song "Standing Up for Nothing," by Caedmon's Call. The song will help them focus on why they need to strive to make an impact on others for the sake of Christ. The song can be found on the group's self-titled album.

REFLECTING ON THE LESSON

Form pairs and have partners take turns telling each other the way they would complete these sentences:

- **One important thing I've learned from this lesson is . . .**
- **One thing I'll do this week to help me apply what I've learned today is . . .**

If you have time, encourage students to tell the whole group how they completed the previous sentences. Then distribute copies of the reproducible student sheet titled "Alien Invasion Challenge" that's found on page 48 of this book. Conclude by saying, **"This week, let God invade your life by taking the challenge written on your sheet. Then tell us all about it next week."**

Close with prayer.

Materials needed:
Reproducible student sheet on page 48 of this book

Alien of the Year Award

This "Alien of the Year" Award is hereby presented to

_____

because of

on behalf of _____ (your name) and the many others who
look to you as a true example of what it means to be a Christian.

Imitate God

Next to each letter below, write one idea that starts with that letter to show how you can imitate God with your assigned people group (families, co-workers, non-Christian friends or Christian friends). Then use scissors to cut apart the sections of your handout.

I.
....

M.
....

I.
....

T.
....

A.
....

T.
....

E.
....

G.
....

O.
....

D.

ALIEN INVASION CHALLENGE

This week, sit down with your family and ask them how you can do a better job of loving and respecting them in your daily life. Do the same with your boss at work, and with your close Christian and non-Christian friends.

Then, at the end of the week, write responses to the questions below:

• How did I show love and respect for others this week?

• Based on my experiences this week, how would my life be different if I made a point of always respecting other people, regardless of how they treat me, for the rest of my life?

ALIEN OPPOSITION 6

In this session, students will form teams to investigate the various pieces of armor and fighting strategies described in Ephesians 6. Then they'll design creative ways to teach each other what they've learned. Through this study, your group will learn why it's important to prepare for spiritual battle every day, and learn ways they can support each other whenever they feel attacked.

LESSON TEXT
Ephesians 6:10-24

LESSON FOCUS
Jesus equips us to stand against Satanic opposition.

LESSON GOALS
As a result of participating in this lesson, students will:
• Discover who their real enemy is.
• Examine the weapons God has provided us for the battle.
• Explore spiritual fighting tactics that really work.

Materials needed:
Blindfolds

Sightings

1 BLIND FACE-OFF

Form pairs and blindfold one of the partners. Have partners stand facing each other, about one foot apart, and have them hold both their hands up as though they were being held at gunpoint. (See the illustration in the margin.) On "go," have students try to knock each other off balance by pressing against the palms of each other's hands. Tell them they can't touch any other part of their partner's body. After they play for one minute, have them switch roles so that the other partner can experience the game blindfolded.

After another minute of play, stop the game. Have partners discuss these questions:

• **Was this game hard? Why or why not?**
• **Did you prefer to play the game with the blindfold or without it? Explain.**

Read Ephesians 6:12. Then ask:

• **How is playing this game blindfolded similar to spiritual warfare in real life?**

Conclude by saying, **"There are a lot of benefits that come with being a Christian. We've talked about many of them during this study. But there is one big drawback. When we joined God's family, we inherited not only his blessings—we also inherited his enemies. As Christian 'aliens' on earth, we now have a supernatural enemy who hates us and has a vast army at his disposal. Fortunately, God has given us supernatural armor and weapons**

that enable us to topple the enemy—if we know how to use them properly. That's what we're going to study today."

WHAT YOU CAN'T SEE CAN HURT YOU

Tape a sheet of newsprint to the wall. Ask students to brainstorm a list of things that can harm you, even through you may not be able to see them with the naked eye. Some examples include cancer, poisonous gas and a sniper.

After you've listed ten items or so, stop and ask:

- **Since we can't see these things, what are some ways we avoid being injured by them?**

Read Ephesians 6:12, then ask:

- **How is our struggle against these "invisible" enemies similar to our struggle against Satan and his forces?**
- **How can we protect ourselves against Satan, even though we can't see him with the naked eye?**

Conclude by saying, "**When we joined God's family, we inherited his enemies, which means that because you've put your trust in Christ, Satan now hates you as much as he hates God. In fact, he wants to destroy your life. Fortunately, God has provided us with spiritual weapons and armor that we can use against Satan. Today we're going to explore how we can use our spiritual armor and weapons to defeat our spiritual enemy.**"

Close Encounters

WARFARE TRAINING 101

Form seven groups (a group can be one person). Have groups read Ephesians 6:10-20. Then assign each group one of the following topics: belt of truth; breastplate of righteousness; feet of readiness; shield of faith; helmet of salvation; sword of the Spirit; and warfare strategy. Set out the supplies listed above, including a variety of Bible study aids, such as a concordance, a Bible dictionary, a Bible encyclopedia and an expository dictionary of biblical words. Then give the groups these instructions: "**Your goal is to use these study aids and the information contained in Ephesians 6:10-20 to learn what your assigned piece of armor really is and how Christians can use it effectively. Then you can use these craft supplies to create a representation of your assigned armor, so you can teach the rest of the class how to use it in daily life.**

"**Warfare strategy team, your goal is to use these same resources to discover two or three really effective strategies for battling against the forces of darkness. Then you'll share those strategies with the rest of the groups.**"

Allow groups 10 to 15 minutes to complete their assignments. Be available to any group that is having trouble using the Bible aids or

---

Materials needed:
Newsprint; masking tape; marker

Check This . . .
If students took the "Alien Invasion Challenge" last week, take a few minutes at the start of the session to have them share their experiences with the group.

Check This . . .
Paul's description of an armored warrior would have likely conjured in his readers' minds images of a Roman soldier ready to do battle. That's because most of the adults who heard this letter would have seen a Roman soldier and could easily relate that image to their own spiritual battles with Satan and his forces.

Materials needed:
Cardboard; newsprint; tape; markers; foil; Bibles; various Bible study aids

---

Check This . . .
If you have fewer than seven students, just have students double up on pieces of armor, or have the whole group work on studying all of the armor pieces together.

Check This . . .
While groups investigate their assigned piece of armor, consider playing some appropriate music in the background. For example, you might play the song "Landmarks," by Plankeye, from their *The One and Only* CD. Also, you could play the song "Much Afraid," on the CD by the same name created by Jars of Clay.

completing their assignment. If students resist the idea of doing an intense Bible study like this, point out that studying the Bible in this way is a part of real spiritual warfare, and it's very important to hone their skills so they'll be more effective in battling the enemy.

Once kids have done their research, have them use the supplies you've provided to create a model of their assigned weapon. (The warfare strategy team will not have to do this part. But you may want to have this team look up another Scripture, 2 Corinthians 10:3-5, at this time.) After students complete their research and create the model of their assigned weapon, encourage them to discuss the best way to present what they've learned to the other groups.

Then have groups discuss these questions:
- **What's hard about doing research like this?**
- **How is doing this kind of Bible study similar to the way a warrior might prepare for battle?**
- **Why is understanding how to study the Bible so important to spiritual warfare?**

Conclude the discussions by saying, **"Studying the Bible is one vital way we can equip ourselves to fight against the enemy. Now let's share with each other what we've learned about other strategies at our disposal and the weapons God has given us."**

WARRIORS IN TRAINING

Distribute writing utensils and copies of the reproducible student sheet found on page 54 of this book. Encourage students to take notes while the other groups present their information. Read through Ephesians 6:10-20, stopping each time you read about one of the pieces of armor that God has provided us. When you stop, have the appropriate team present its information. After you read the entire passage, have the warfare strategy team share its information. Once everyone has had a chance to make their presentation, discuss these questions:
- **What might an attack from the enemy look like in real life?**
- **How can you recognize when the enemy is attacking you? your friends?**
- **What can you do every day to help you be ready for any attack that the enemy might launch against you?**

Conclude by saying, **"Take your sheet home and study it this week as you read through Ephesians 6. Practice putting on your armor and going to battle against the enemy. Remember, now that you're a Christian, Satan will attack you. It's to your benefit to be ready for the attack when it comes."**

A LESSON FROM HISTORY

Read aloud the following quote to your students, but don't tell them who you're quoting.

"These are the times that try men's souls. The summer soldier and the sunshine patriot will, in this crisis, shrink

Materials needed:
Supplies from previous activity; Bibles; writing utensils; reproducible student sheet on page 54 of this book

Materials needed:
Bibles

from the service of their country; but he that stands it *now* deserves the love and thanks of man and woman. Tyranny, like hell, is not easily conquered; yet we have this consolation with us, that the harder the conflict, the more glorious the triumph. What we obtain too cheap, we esteem too lightly; it is dearness only that gives every thing its value. Heaven knows how to put a proper price upon its goods; and it would be strange indeed if so celestial an article as FREEDOM should not be highly rated . . . .

"I love the man that can smile in trouble, that can gather strength from distress, and grow brave by reflection. 'Tis the business of little minds to shrink; but he whose heart is firm, and whose conscience approves his conduct, will pursue his principles unto death."[1]

After the reading, ask:

- **Who do you think said this?**
- **In what circumstance might it have been spoken?**

Have a volunteer read Ephesians 6:10-20. Then ask:

- **How is this quote similar to Paul's words in Ephesians?**
- **What does this quote have to say about spiritual warfare?**

Comment, **"This quote was originally spoken by Thomas Paine to a gathering of American troops during the American Revolution. But even though his words were spoken about physical war, the truths can also be applied to our present-day spiritual struggle."**

Ask:

- **How is spiritual warfare a struggle for true freedom?**
- **What do you think would happen if you ignored the spiritual war going on around you?**

Conclude by saying, **"Spiritual warfare is real—just as real as the physical war Thomas Paine and the American troops faced so many years ago. But our war is different. It cannot be seen with the naked eye. And that can sometimes make us lazy and choose not to fight. Remember, Satan wants to destroy your life. But God has provided ample protection for you, through these weapons we have studied. Learn to use them every day. And you, too, will learn what it really means to be free."**

Life Invasion

ON THE ATTACK

Hang the pieces of armor your students created onto one of the meeting room walls. Gather your group around the armor and say, **"One of the strategies for effective warfare that Paul suggests is to pray for each other. Let's close today by going to battle for one another in prayer."**

Have students each turn to a partner and share one prayer request they have that they would like someone to pray for. Then have pairs

Materials needed:
Armor pieces students created earlier; tape or pushpins

pray together, asking God to answer the prayer requests they've shared, and asking him to help them become effective spiritual warriors for God.

Close the prayer time by quoting Ephesians 6:23, 24 which says, **"Peace to the brothers, and love with faith from God the Father and the Lord Jesus Christ. Grace to all who love our Lord Jesus Christ with an undying love."**

REFLECTING ON THE LESSON

Form pairs and have partners take turns telling each other the way they would complete these sentences:

- **One important thing I've learned from this lesson is . . .**
- **One thing I'll do this week to help me apply what I've learned today is . . .**

If you have time, encourage students to tell the whole group how they completed the previous sentences. Then distribute copies of the reproducible student sheet titled "Alien Invasion Challenge" that's found on page 55 of this book. Conclude by saying, **"This week, let God invade your life by taking the challenge written on your sheet. Then tell us all about it next week."**

Close with prayer.

Materials needed:
Reproducible student sheet on page 55 of this book

Warfare training 101

◆ **B**elt of truth:

◆ **B**reastplate of righteousness:

◆ **S**hoes of readiness:

◆ **S**hield of faith:

◆ **h**elmet of salvation:

◆ **S**word of the Spirit:

◆ **W**arfare strategies:

ALIEN INVASION CHALLENGE

This week, spend 20 minutes every morning prayerfully reading through Ephesians 6:10-20, and mentally "put on" the armor of God before you face the day. During the day, take time to pray as you walk between classes or over your lunch break, asking God to help you recognize spiritual attacks, and learn how to fight against them.

Then, at the end of the week, write responses to the questions below:

• How did I participate in spiritual warfare this week?

• Based on my experiences this week, how would my life be different if I practiced putting on the armor of God for the rest of my life?

STRATEGIC INVASION

After you've finished the six sessions in this book, give your teenagers a chance to put what they've learned into action through this creative real-world "invasion." Your students will form alien hit squads that will each come up with a secret one-day attack plan for spreading God's love to others in a creative way. For example, the "families" hit squad might create care-package "bombs" to drop on the front steps of each group member's home (where the parents will find it). Or, the "non-Christian" hit squad might create invitations to a special youth event for non-Christians that your group will help design and lead. The only catch is that what students do must be covert, so that families and friends don't know where the care package (or the invitation) came from until a later date.

Focus

This is a special event—a pre-planned "strategic" invasion that students create and execute as a way to advance God's kingdom in each of the following areas:
- their families
- their co-workers
- their non-Christian friends
- their Christian friends

1 Before the Invasion

Near the end of your six-week study, invite your teenagers to a special meeting to discuss this creative way they can put what they've learned into practice by secretly "invading" your church and community. At this special meeting, divide the group into four teams: Families, Co-workers, Christian friends and Non-Christian friends. Then have each team brainstorm some creative ways that they might secretly "invade" their assigned group with a demonstration of God's love. Use the suggestions on pages 58, 59 to help spark ideas, but let your teens ultimately decide what they want to do. Once the groups decide on a plan of action, have teams assign various responsibilities to each team member. For example, you might need some students to collect supplies, create crafts or make phone calls. Make sure every person is directly involved in some way.

Once the responsibilities have been assigned, work with your group to set a date for the "invasion." Create a detailed schedule for the day's events—including:
- where you will meet to start the day
- who will make sure all the necessary supplies are ready to go
- who will drive the various groups to their designated invasion sites
- how each invasion team will carry out its task

- where the teams will meet after the invasion to celebrate their success

2 The Day of the Invasion

When the big day arrives, invite students to arrive early for a time of prayer and spiritual warfare. Read through Ephesians 6:10-20 again, and encourage your teens to put on their spiritual armor as they prepare to invade the world with God's love. Also use this time to take care of any last-minute details. Then, when everything is ready, launch the invasion.

After the invasion, have teens meet at a designated location for a celebration. At some point during the celebration, lead them to discuss the following questions:

- **How does it feel to accomplish what you did today?**
- **Through this strategic invasion, how have you followed the teachings we've studied in Ephesians over the past several weeks?**
- **What do you hope that people will gain from the way we "invaded" their lives today?**
- **What did you gain today?**
- **Do you think you've changed because of this study? Why or why not?**
- **Will your life be any different as a result of the study and today's experience? Why or why not?**
- **Based on today's experience, what's one change you really want to see happen in your life?**
- **What do you need from this group to help you apply what we've learned in this study to your life from now on?**

After the discussion, let your students share how they've seen other group members grow or change as a result of this study and today's experience. Once again, congratulate them on their efforts and encourage them to let this experience become the launching point for a lifetime of planning "strategic invasions" of God's love into other people's lives.

3 Idea-Starters for Types of "Strategic Invasions"

Here are some creative options your teens might consider as each group plans its "strategic invasion" into the world.

STRATEGIES FOR THE "FAMILIES" TEAM

• Drop care-package "bombs" onto the doorsteps of group members' families. Include sweets, recipes, parenting books or coupons for local businesses.
• Invite families to a special "Father/Daughter" or "Mother/Son" talent show that teens plan and lead at the church.
• Totally clean the house when no one is around. When your parents ask you about it, try not to give yourself away.

STRATEGIES FOR THE "CO-WORKERS" TEAM

• Bring surprise treats that you make yourself for everyone at your workplace.
• Write a note of appreciation to your boss, but don't sign it. Instead, secretly plant it on his or her desk, and let your boss try to figure out who wrote it.
• Buy or make a little gift for each of your co-workers, then secretly deliver it to them without letting them see you.

STRATEGIES FOR THE "NON-CHRISTIAN FRIENDS" TEAM

• Cover their car with invitations to your youth group, but don't leave your name. Instead, sign the cards, "God."
• Write a note to one or more of your non-Christian friends, telling them what you admire about their lives. Then plant the note in their locker at school, so they'll find it at a later date.
• Secretly wash their car, then leave a note on the windshield that says, "This act of kindness has been done by a friend of yours to brighten your day and remind you in a small way that God loves you."

STRATEGIES FOR THE "CHRISTIAN FRIENDS" TEAM

• Pool your money together and purchase a gift certificate to your pastor's favorite restaurant. Deliver the certificate to his house, along with a note that simply says, "Jesus loves you."
• Write special notes of encouragement to other group members who are not on your team and secretly deliver them to their homes while they're out doing other things.
• Make special treats for everyone in your group, then bring them to the celebration at the end of the invasion, so everybody can enjoy them together. Don't tell anyone where the treats came from.

Notes

LESSON 1

[1]John J. Kohut & Roland Sweet, *Dumb, Dumber, Dumbest* (New York: Penguin Books, 1996), p. 69.

LESSON 2

[1]*Illustrations Unlimited*, ed. by James S. Hewett (Wheaton, IL: Tyndale House Publishers, 1997), pp. 221, 222.

LESSON 4

[1]*Illustrations Unlimited*, ed. by James S. Hewett (Wheaton, IL: Tyndale House Publishers, 1997), pp. 123, 124.

LESSON 5

[1]*Illustrations Unlimited*, ed. by James S. Hewett (Wheaton, IL: Tyndale House Publishers, 1997), pp. 324, 325.

LESSON 6

[1]*The Book of Wisdom* (Sisters, OR: Multnomah Books, 1997), p. 26.

OtHEr EmpOweRed YouTh PrODuCts frOm StANdaRd PubLiShiNG

SOME KIND OF JOURNEY
VIDEO CURRICULUM

This innovative video curriculum is divided into seven segments perfect for youth group discussion. Included with the 90-minute video is a leader's guide to help you challenge your teens to grapple with the same issues that are discussed on the video—things like absolutes, swearing, homosexuality. Also included is a coupon good for $2.00 off any number of copies of the companion book, *SOME KIND OF JOURNEY: ON the Road With Audio Adrenaline.*

Order # 03318
(UPC 7-07529-03318-1)

SOME KIND OF JOURNEY
ON THE ROAD WITH AUDIO ADRENALINE

By Jim Burgen, Ginny McCabe and Dale Reeves

Seven strangers from across the country spent a week on the road with one of today's hottest Christian bands, Audio Adrenaline. Why? To talk about seven relevant issues that concern today's youth—such as depression, sex, prejudice and divorce. Includes an AudioVision CD with interactive discussions, songs, videos and more! You'll also get behind-the-scenes tour photos of the band and the seven people who journeyed with them.

Order # 03304
(ISBN 0-7847-0744-8)

NO ACCIDENT . . . NO APOLOGIES
Helping Teens Understand the Creation/Evolution Debate

By Geoff Moore and Jim Eichenberger

This six-session video curriculum features a 40-minute video hosted by contemporary Christian artist Geoff Moore. Guide your teens in exploring what the Bible says about the creation account and the importance of standing boldly for God in their schools. In addition to a leader's guide, reproducible student sheets and a bonus music video are also included.

Order # 03308 (ISBN 0-7847-0788-X)

WHY BE NORMAL?
A Creative Study of the Sermon on the Mount

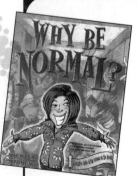

By Michael Warden

This six-session elective for junior-high and senior-high teens will help them ignite their world by living out Christ's challenge in Matthew 5-7. Each session features reproducible student sheets, contemporary Christian music suggestions, numerous options and a midweek challenge. A bonus event gives youth the opportunity to "take the dare" and share Christ publicly.

Order # 23309
(ISBN 0-7847-0769-3)

X-TREME ALTITUDE
A Creative Study of the Book of Nehemiah

By Sheila Corey

This six-session elective for senior-high teens will help students overcome the obstacles they encounter as they construct a stronger faith in God. Each session features reproducible student sheets, contemporary Christian music suggestions, a midweek guide for personal devotions and numerous options! Also includes a bonus event—a party for underprivileged kids, put on by your students!

Order # 23311
(ISBN 0-7847-0761-8)

TO ORDER, CONTACT YOUR LOCAL CHRISTIAN BOOKSTORE.
(IF THE BOOK IS OUT OF STOCK, YOU CAN ORDER BY CALLING 1-800-543-1353.)